ARE YOU WITH US OR AGAINST US?

Looking Back at the Reign of Terror History 6th Grade

Children's European History

The French Revolution took place between 1789 and
1798. It was exciting, violent, scary, and led to both
good things and bad things for France and its people.
One bad thing was the Reign of Terror. What was it?
Why did it happen? Read on and find out!

THE FRENCH REVOLUTION

Before the French Revolution, France was governed by a king and controlled by the nobility and the very rich. The gap between rich and poor was so extreme that the ordinary people fought to take power out of the hands of the wealthy and powerful.

King Louis XVI

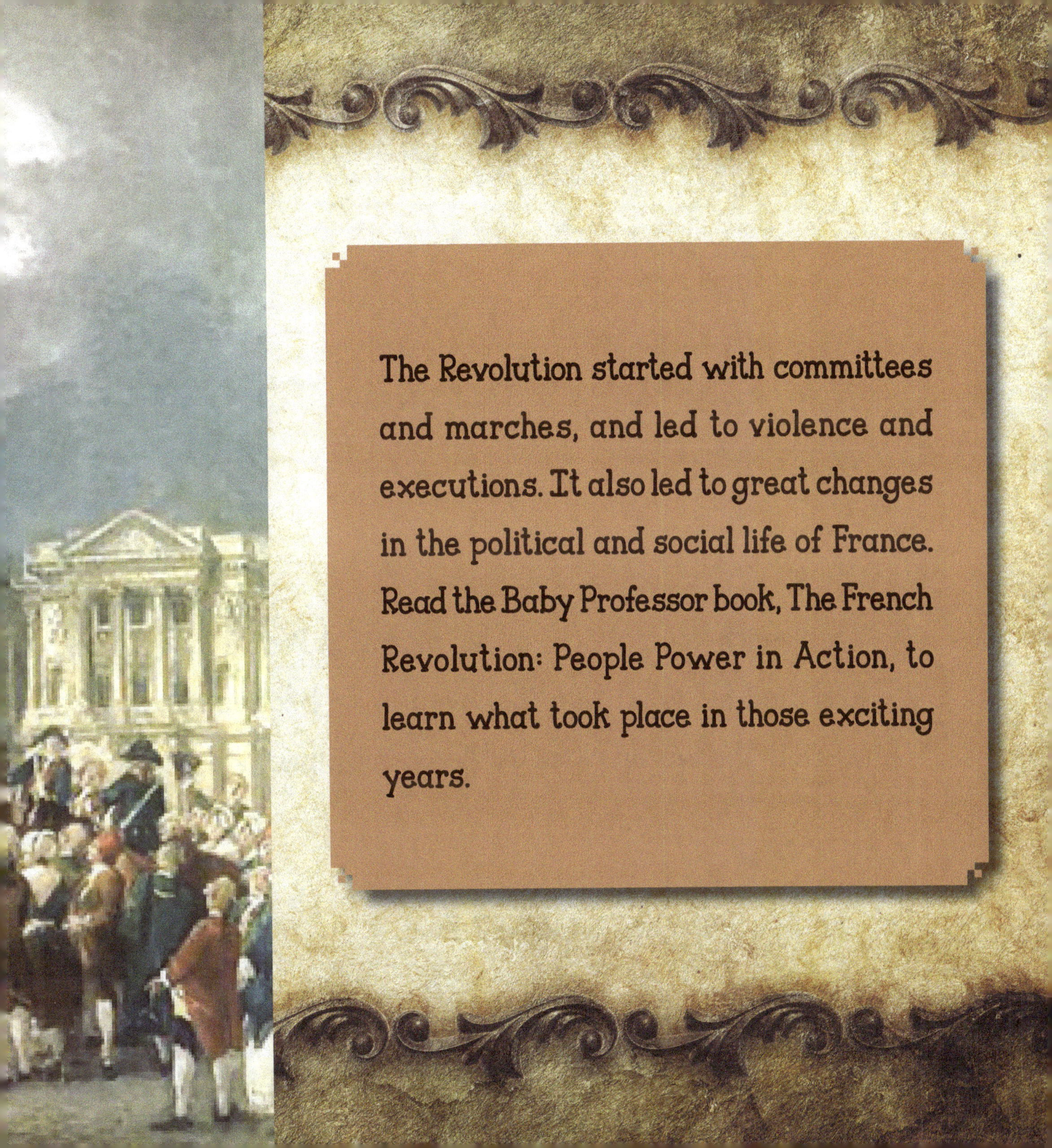

The Revolution started with committees and marches, and led to violence and executions. It also led to great changes in the political and social life of France. Read the Baby Professor book, The French Revolution: People Power in Action, to learn what took place in those exciting years.

ENEMIES NEAR AND FAR AWAY

The French Revolution was not peaceful. People fought and died for what they believed in, or because they were in the wrong place at the wrong time.

LIBERTÉ

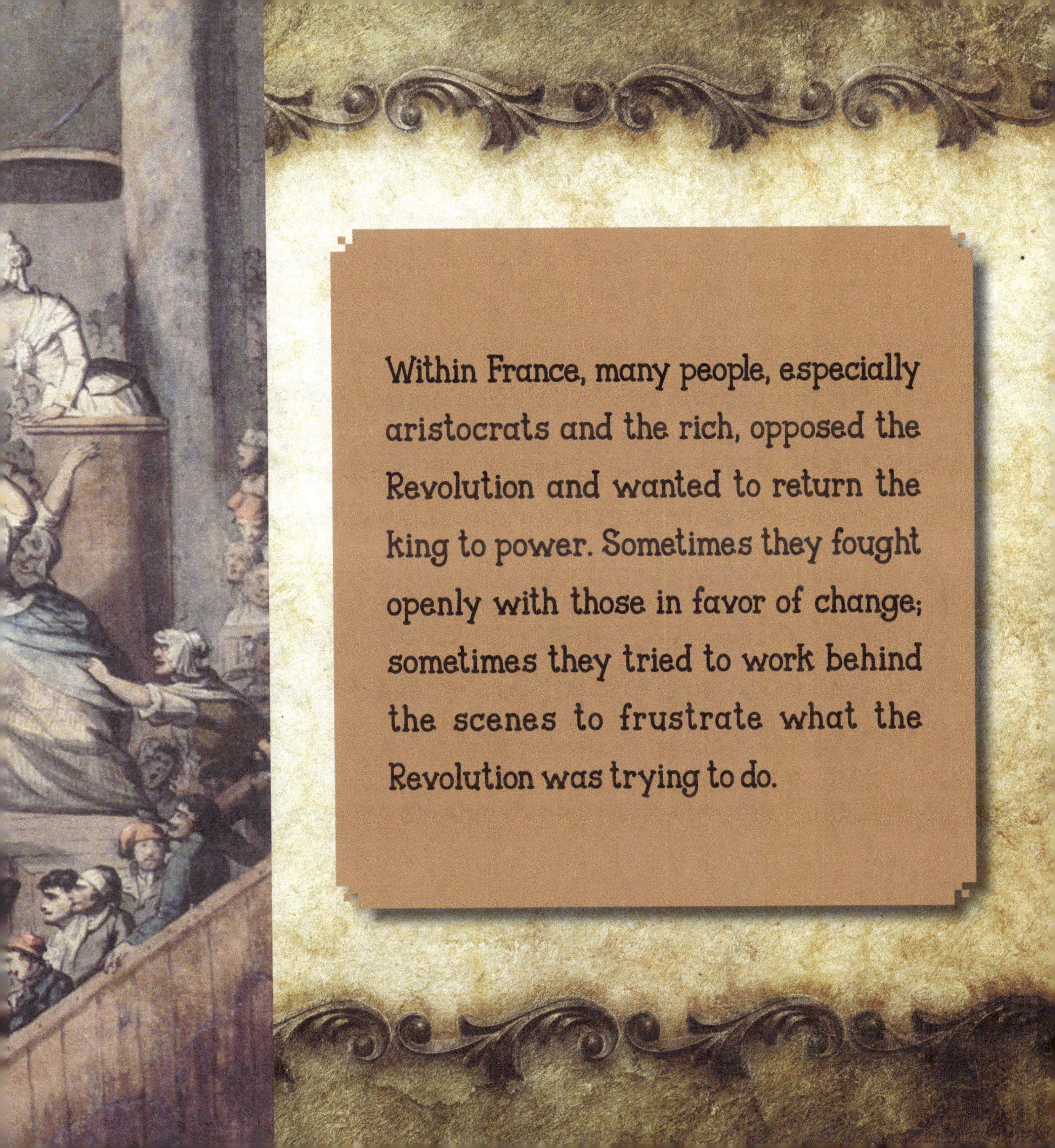

Within France, many people, especially aristocrats and the rich, opposed the Revolution and wanted to return the king to power. Sometimes they fought openly with those in favor of change; sometimes they tried to work behind the scenes to frustrate what the Revolution was trying to do.

On the side of the Revolution, many people acted on anger and need that had been building up for decades. The rich were just too rich, and everyone else had barely enough to survive. Mobs stormed the houses of the rich and large landowners, took everything they could find, and burned the houses. Sometimes they killed the owners of the houses.

Fighting at the Hotel de Ville

The nobility had been used to absolute power for hundreds of years. When that power was taken away, they found themselves arrested, in prison, or even executed. The government took their wealth to support the army, to feed the poor, and to fund other changes in the way France was run.

FOREIGN THREATS

Outside of France, other countries were offended and worried by the French Revolution. Almost every other country in Europe at that time had a king, and the leaders of those countries were afraid that the ideas of the French Revolution would spread across France's borders. Some countries also saw an opportunity, since France was distracted with internal struggles. Prussia and Austria, in particular prepared to invade France, both to restore the French king and to strengthen their own positions.

France government

SHORTAGE OF MONEY, SHORTAGE OF FOOD

France was deeply in debt, due to bad decisions by the government under the previous kings. As well, a drought led to several years of bad harvests. There was little food, and the people had little money so there was not much for the tax collectors to collect. The nobility strongly rejected using any of their wealth to support the country.

DIVISIONS IN THE REVOLUTION

The Revolution faced challenges from those who wanted to restore the king, and threats from other countries. But there were also struggles within the leadership of the Revolution. There were more moderate factions, like the Girondins, and more extreme factions like the Jacobins.

Banquet of the Girondins

Girondins

THE GIRONDINS

The "moderates" leading the French Revolution still wanted extreme changes in the way the country was governed. In general, they wanted a constitutional monarchy, a system like that of Great Britain. In such a system there is still a king, but the monarchy has limited powers. The main power is held by an assembly of elected representatives.

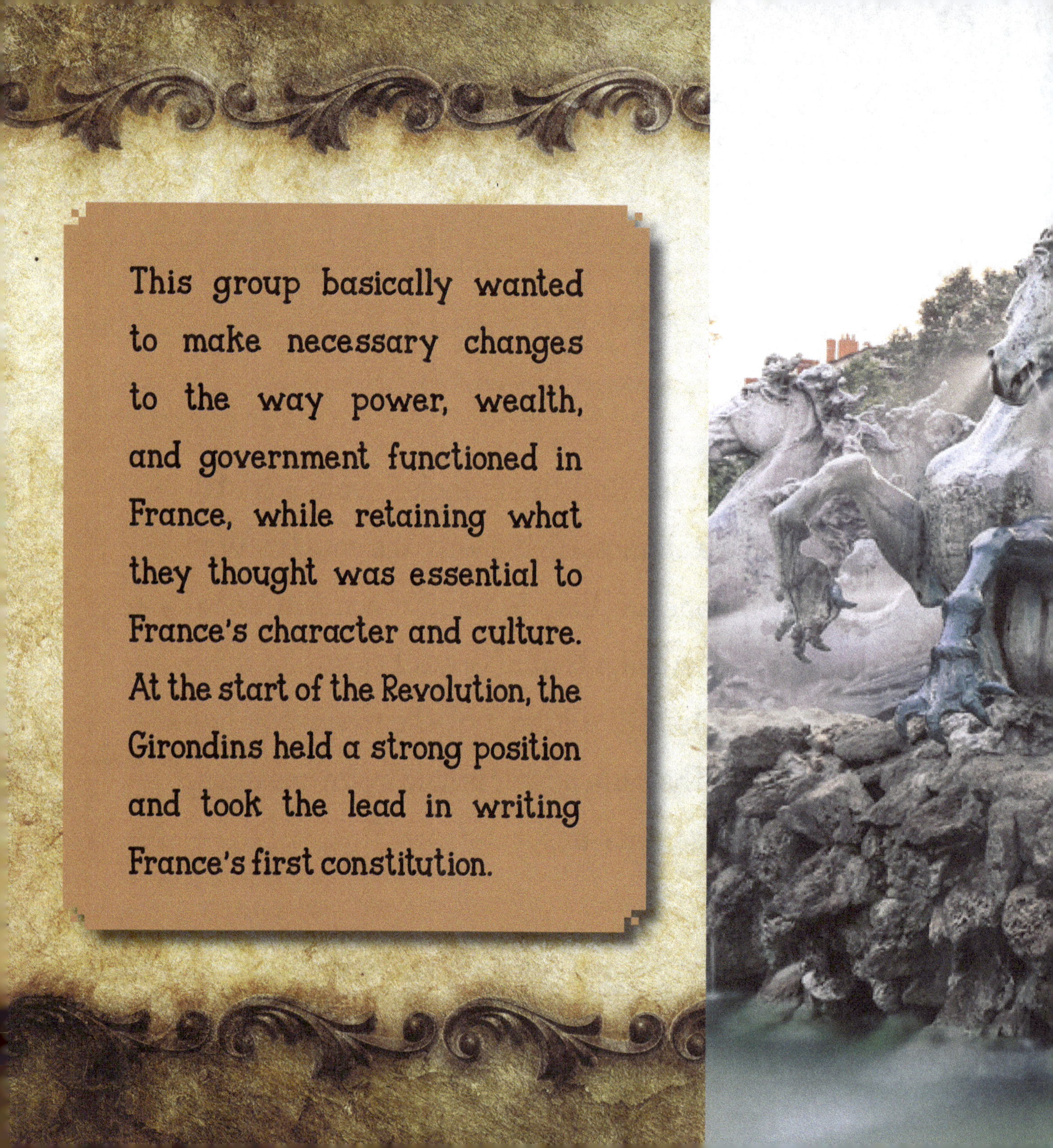

This group basically wanted to make necessary changes to the way power, wealth, and government functioned in France, while retaining what they thought was essential to France's character and culture. At the start of the Revolution, the Girondins held a strong position and took the lead in writing France's first constitution.

Monument of the Girondins

Maximilien de Robespierre

THE JACOBINS

The more extreme elements of the Revolution included some of its most prominent thinkers and speakers, like Jean-Paul Marat and Maximilien Robespierre. They felt that the whole political and cultural system of France needed to be overturned so that a government "of the people" could emerge. Some groups on this side of the Revolution felt that violence and killing were not only right to help the Revolution succeed, but were a duty: every true revolutionary should be ready to crack an enemy's head or burn down his house.

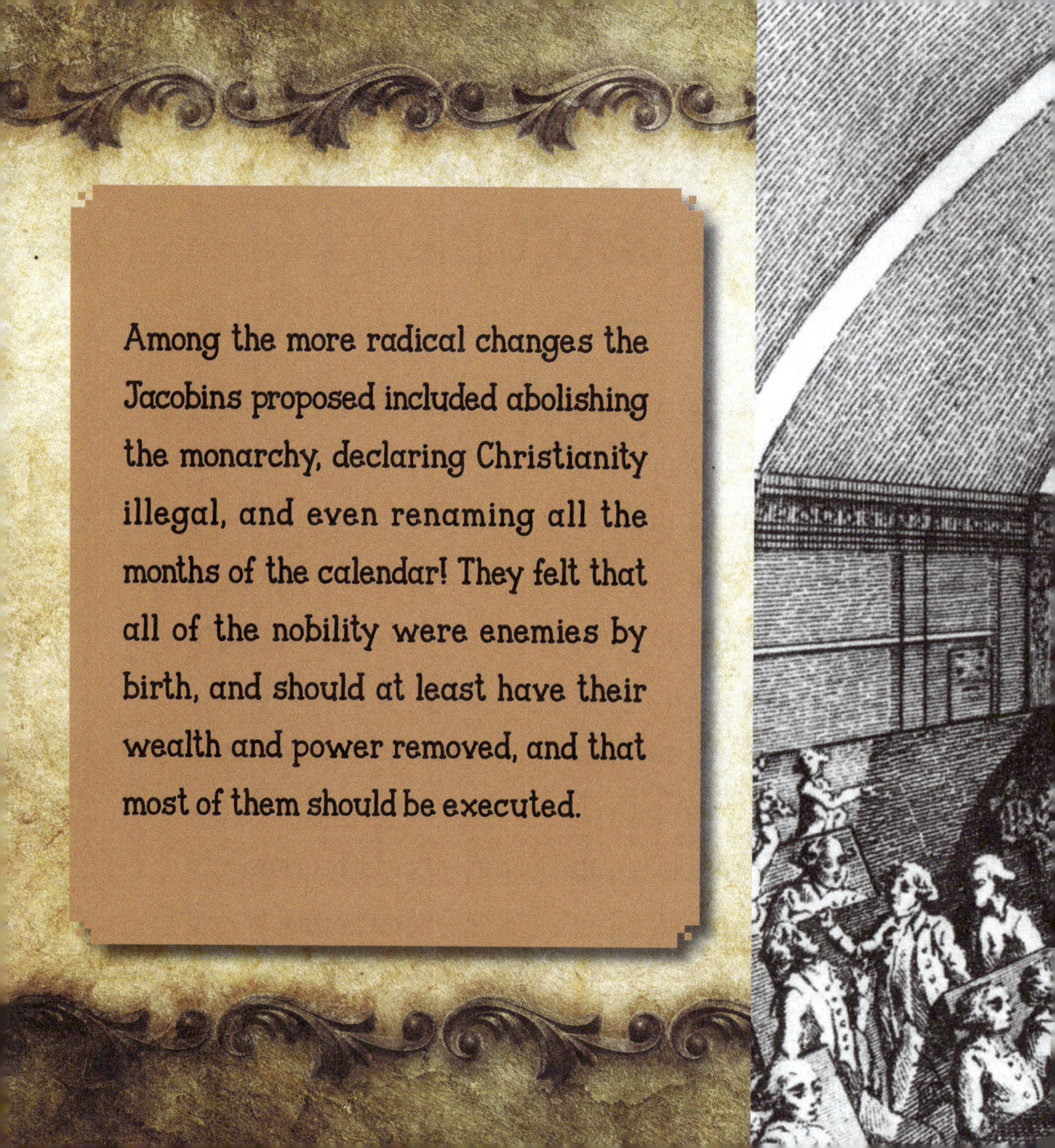

Among the more radical changes the Jacobins proposed included abolishing the monarchy, declaring Christianity illegal, and even renaming all the months of the calendar! They felt that all of the nobility were enemies by birth, and should at least have their wealth and power removed, and that most of them should be executed.

Club of the Jacobins

Charlotte Corday

SLAUGHTER

The balance of power changed through violence. Jacobins attacked and murdered hundreds of Girondists, including members of the government. Some Jacobins paid a price for this: Charlotte Corday, a Girondin supporter, went to the House of Jacobin writer and leader Marat and stabbed him to death.

THE COMMITTEE OF PUBLIC SAFETY

The radical leaders came to see enemies everywhere, even when the threats from foreign countries became less and the king, having been executed, was no longer around. They became convinced that mysterious forces, some within the leadership of the Revolution, were working to make the struggle fail.

Committee of Public Safety

Maximilien de Robespierre

Robespierre also thought that violence was a necessary part of the struggle. He said that, in peacetime, the power of the country rests on virtue. But in times of revolution, you have to add terror to virtue.

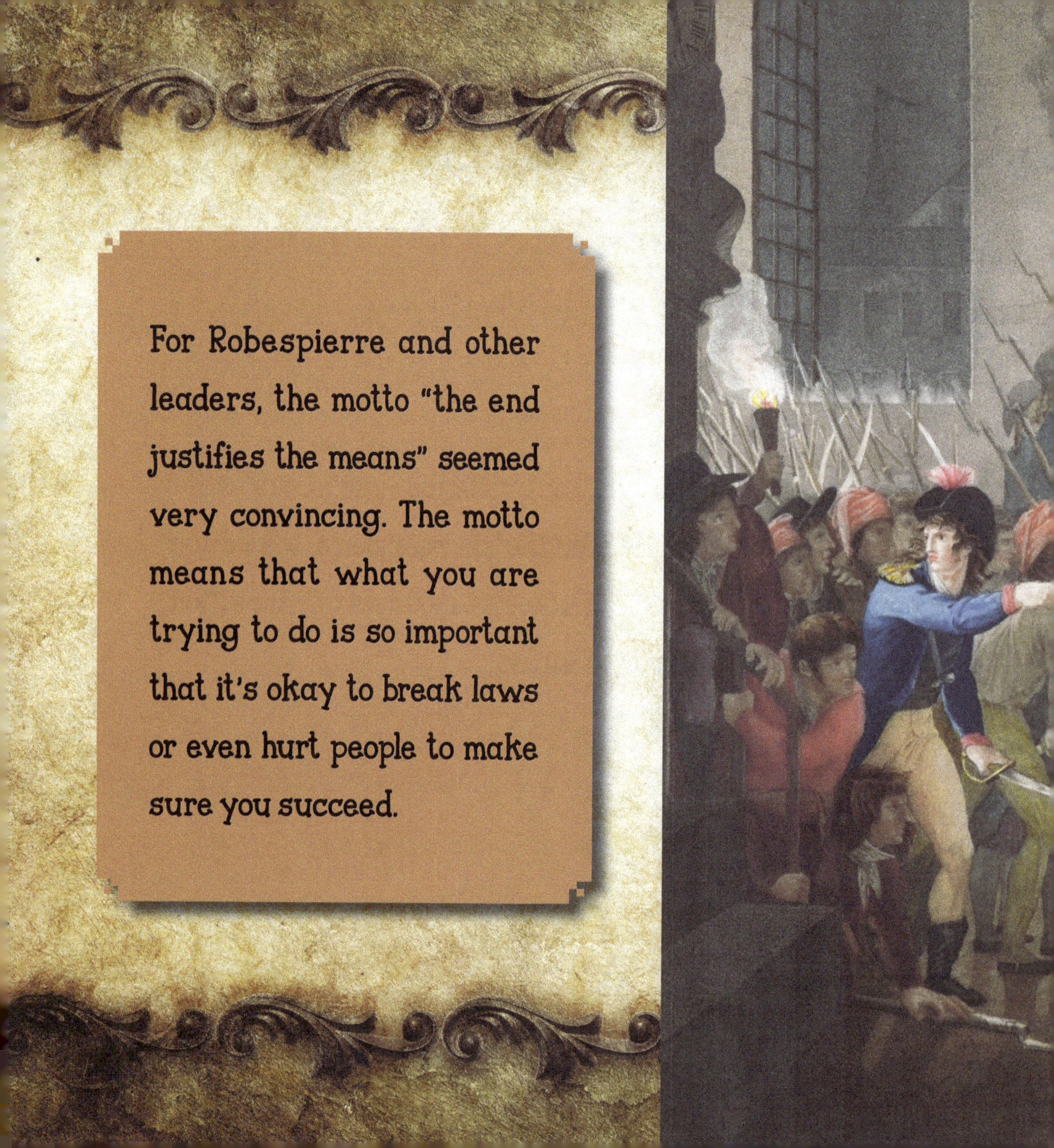

For Robespierre and other leaders, the motto "the end justifies the means" seemed very convincing. The motto means that what you are trying to do is so important that it's okay to break laws or even hurt people to make sure you succeed.

DECLARATION DES DROITS
de l'Homme et du Citoyen

Forming the National Assembly

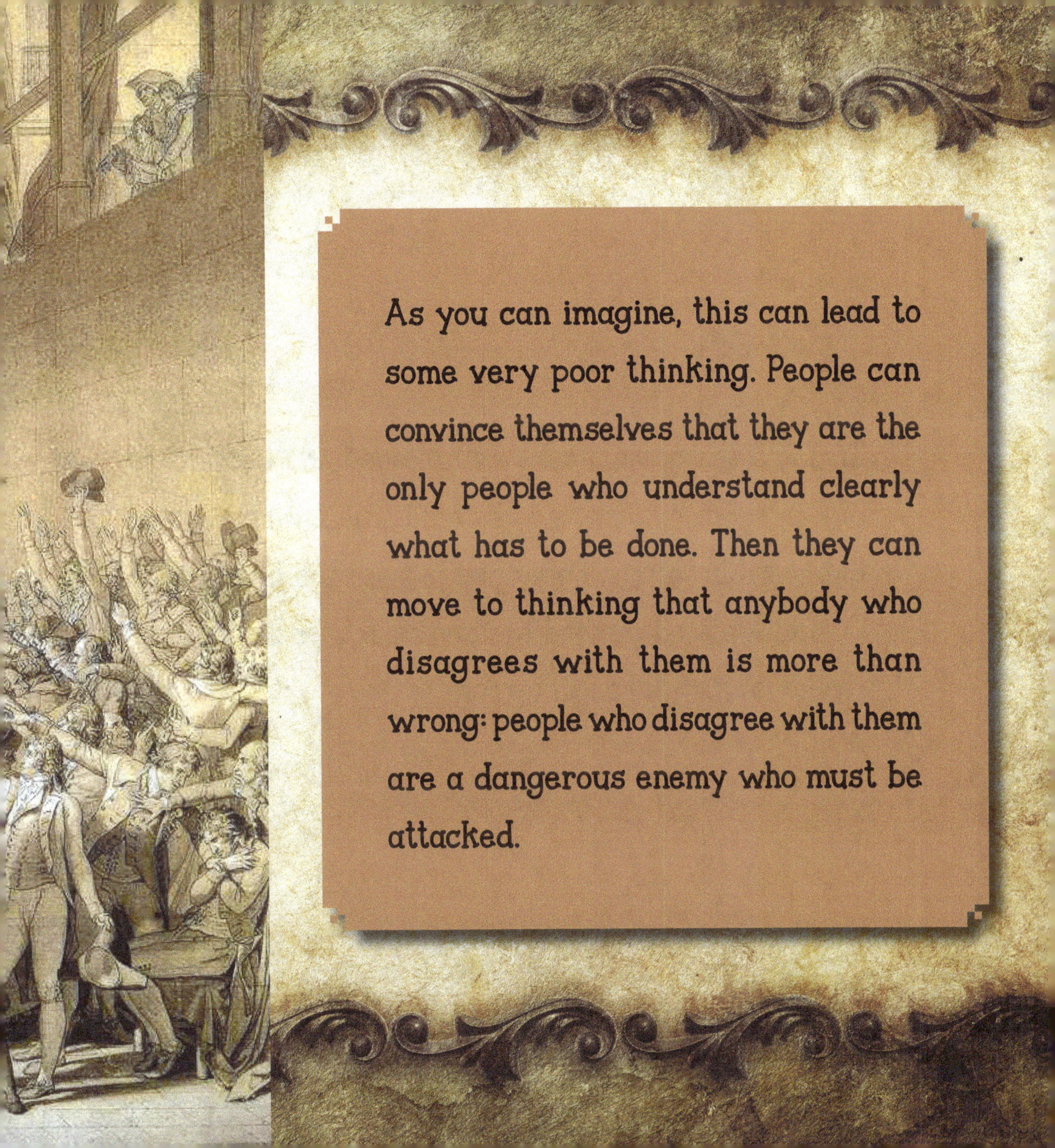

As you can imagine, this can lead to some very poor thinking. People can convince themselves that they are the only people who understand clearly what has to be done. Then they can move to thinking that anybody who disagrees with them is more than wrong: people who disagree with them are a dangerous enemy who must be attacked.

In 1793 the government established the Committee of Public Safety. That's a pleasant title for a body that did horrible things. Robespierre was the head of the Committee, and pushed his argument for supporting the Revolution through terror.

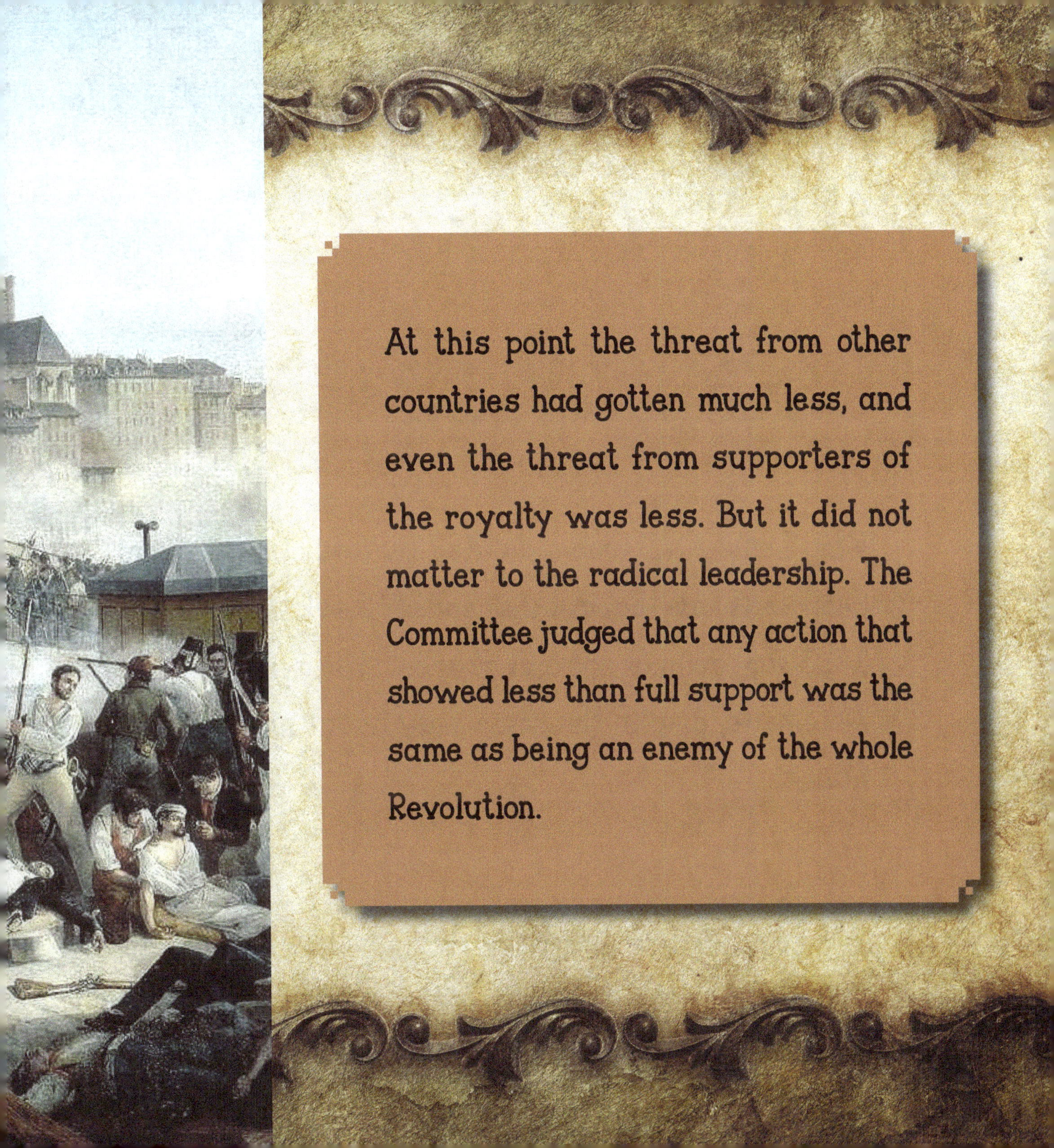

At this point the threat from other countries had gotten much less, and even the threat from supporters of the royalty was less. But it did not matter to the radical leadership. The Committee judged that any action that showed less than full support was the same as being an enemy of the whole Revolution.

THE REIGN OF TERROR

King Louis XVI was executed by guillotine, a huge chopping blade that cut the head off its victim, in early 1793 for "crimes against France". His wife, Marie-Antoinette, died in the same way about nine months later.

Execution of Louis XVI

Our image of the Reign of Terror is of a prince or a duke, stripped of his fancy clothes, being led out to execution in front of a mob. Huge crowds did turn out to see the guillotine at work, and the government encouraged this because it felt seeing this horrible punishment was educational! But of the victims during this time, fewer than 10% were aristocrats.

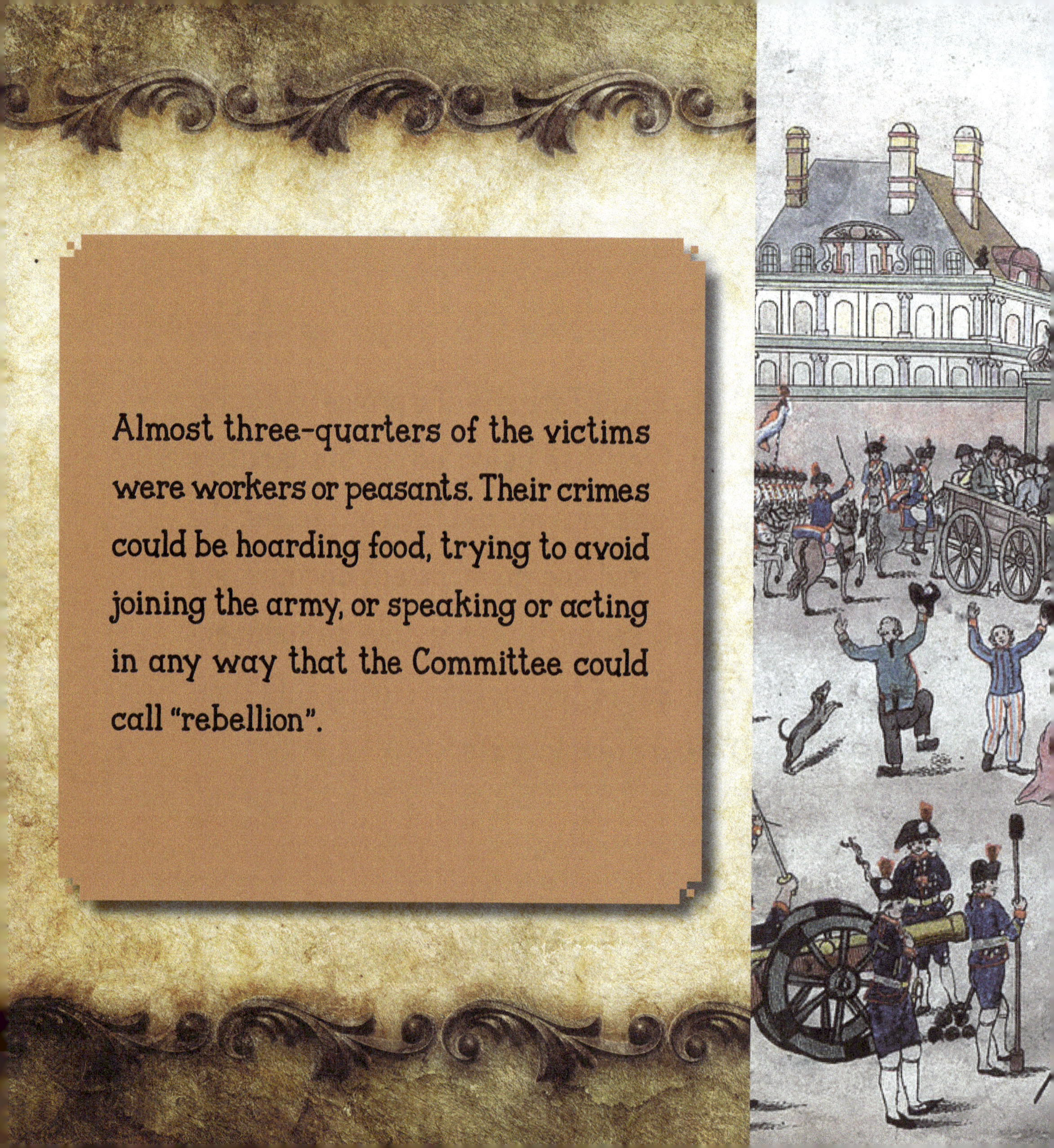

Almost three-quarters of the victims were workers or peasants. Their crimes could be hoarding food, trying to avoid joining the army, or speaking or acting in any way that the Committee could call "rebellion".

The guillotine became the method of execution

Exécution of Marie Antoinette

Across France, about 20,000 people were executed.
Many thousands more were thrown into horrible jails
and died before they could be brought to trial.

You could be arrested because a neighbor said you had made a joke about the Committee. You could be arrested because you owned a lot of land. You could be arrested because you favored some government policy that was different from what the Jacobins favored. You could be arrested for being a Christian. You could be arrested at random, because the Committee thought that would terrify the people around you and convince them to be obedient.

Convent of the Jacobins

The Girondists

As you can see, the Reign of Terror had little or nothing to do with the high ideals (democracy, freedom of thought, equal opportunity) with which the Revolution started!

THE END OF THE TERROR

There was growing resistance throughout the country, not to the Revolution itself, but to the Committee and its Reign of Terror. The other leaders of the government saw that Robespierre's extreme actions could put the whole Revolution at risk.

French Revolution

Arrest of Robespierre

So, when Robespierre called for even more arrests and executions in 1794, and even threatened some of the other members of the Committee of Public Safety, the committee had Robespierre himself arrested. He himself was the last victim of the Reign of Terror.

MORE ABOUT THE FRENCH REVOLUTION

The French Revolution is a big story, full of heroes, villains, and amazing events. Read Baby Professor books like Marquis de Lafayette: A Hero of Two Worlds, Moms Needed Bread!, and They Got Involved! to find out even more.

The Reign of Terror

Visit
BABY PROFESSOR
EDUCATION KIDS
www.BabyProfessorBooks.com
to download Free Baby Professor eBooks
and view our catalog of new and exciting
Children's Books